Cambridge Early Years

Let's Explore

Learner's Book 2B

Kathryn Harper & Elly Schottman

Contents

Note to parents and practitioners   3

Block 3: Working and playing together   4

Block 4: Wonderful water   18

Acknowledgements   32

Note to parents and practitioners

This Learner's Book provides activities to support the second term of Let's Explore for Cambridge Early Years 2.

Activities can be used at school or at home. Children will need support from an adult. Additional guidance about activities can be found in the **For practitioners** boxes.

Some activities use stickers. The stickers can be found in the section in the middle of this book.

Stories are provided for children to enjoy looking at and listening to. Children are not expected to be able to read the stories themselves.

Children will encounter the following characters within this book. You could ask children to point to the characters when they see them on the pages, and say their names.

The Learner's Book activities support the Teaching Resource activities. The Teaching Resource provides step-by-step coverage of the Cambridge Early Years curriculum and guidance on how the Learner's Book activities develop the curriculum learning statements.

Hi, my name is Mia.

Find us on the front covers doing lots of fun activities.

Hi, my name is Gemi.

Hi, my name is Rafi.

Hi, my name is Kiho.

Block 3 — Working and playing together

Group play!
Choose stickers and say.

What do you like to do?
Draw and say.

For practitioners
Discuss the pictures and ask if the children have ever tried these activities. Did they enjoy them?
Children look at the pictures again and draw happy faces next to the indoor and outdoor activities they have tried.

Are they keeping safe?
Spot the difference.

For practitioners
Children examine the two pictures and circle the differences.
Talk about the differences. In which picture are the children keeping safe? Why?

Using our bodies
Join the dots.

For practitioners
Children join the dots to complete each picture. Ask *What other activities do you use your body for? What parts of your body do you use to do these activities?* Talk about the role of body parts in each activity in the pictures and how the children are using them to turn the rope faster or go faster on the scooter, for example.

Movement maze
Follow the lines.

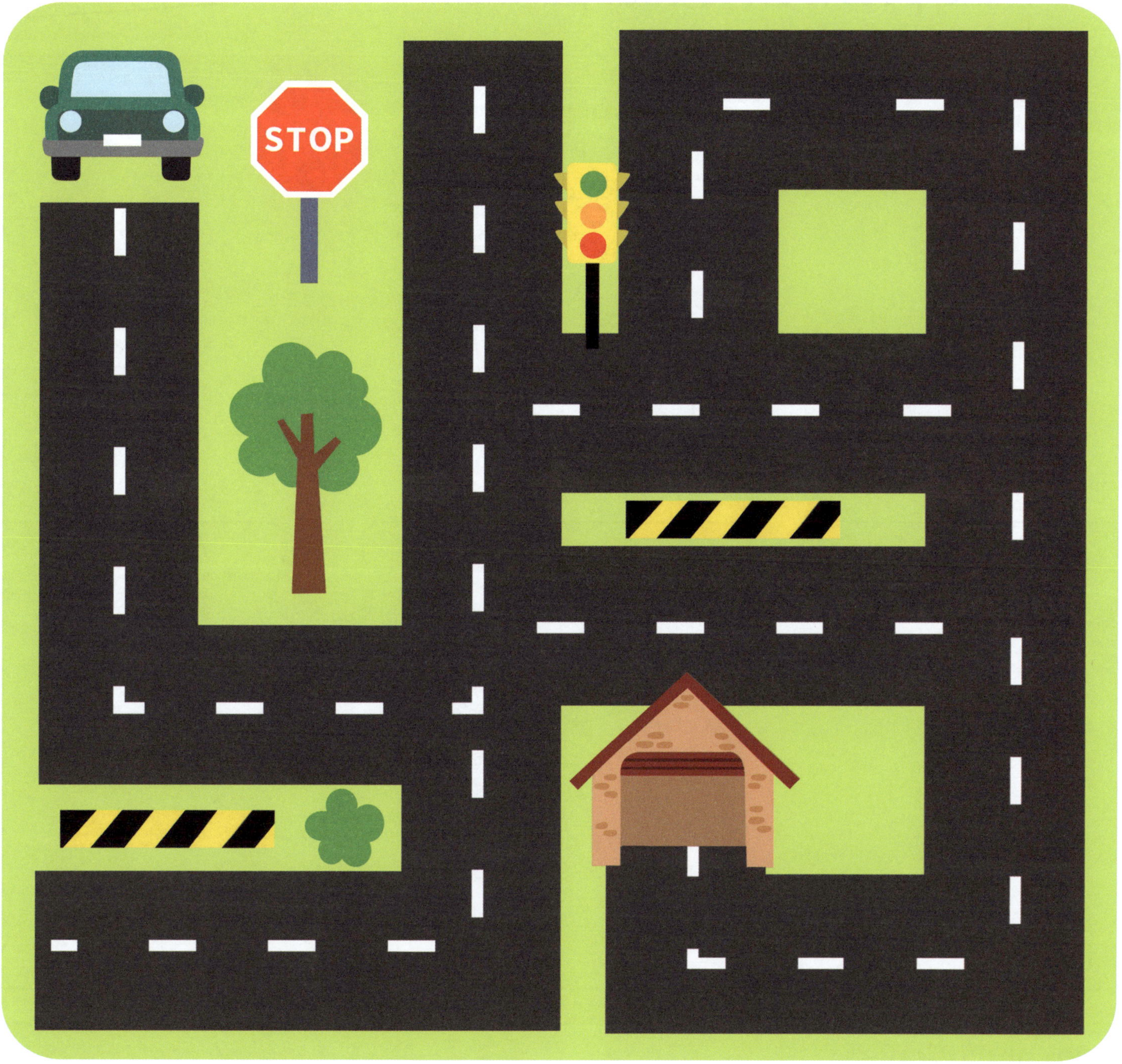

For practitioners
Children work in pairs and use a toy car, or any toy vehicle, to move through the maze to the garage.
One child can give directions while the other child moves the car using directions such as *forwards*, *backwards* and *turn*.

Making a puzzle

Create.

Draw and pass it on to your partner.

For practitioners

Children work in pairs. Explain that they need to decide what picture to draw and who will draw what. The puzzle will be most effective if children collaboratively draw a simple object such as a flower or a teddy bear. Children should take it in turns to each draw in the squares to make up the whole picture of their chosen object. Children can then colour in their picture together. If children are finding it difficult to share the puzzle, help them to work together. You could help them to decide what the picture on the puzzle should be.

What's that sound?
Colour and say.

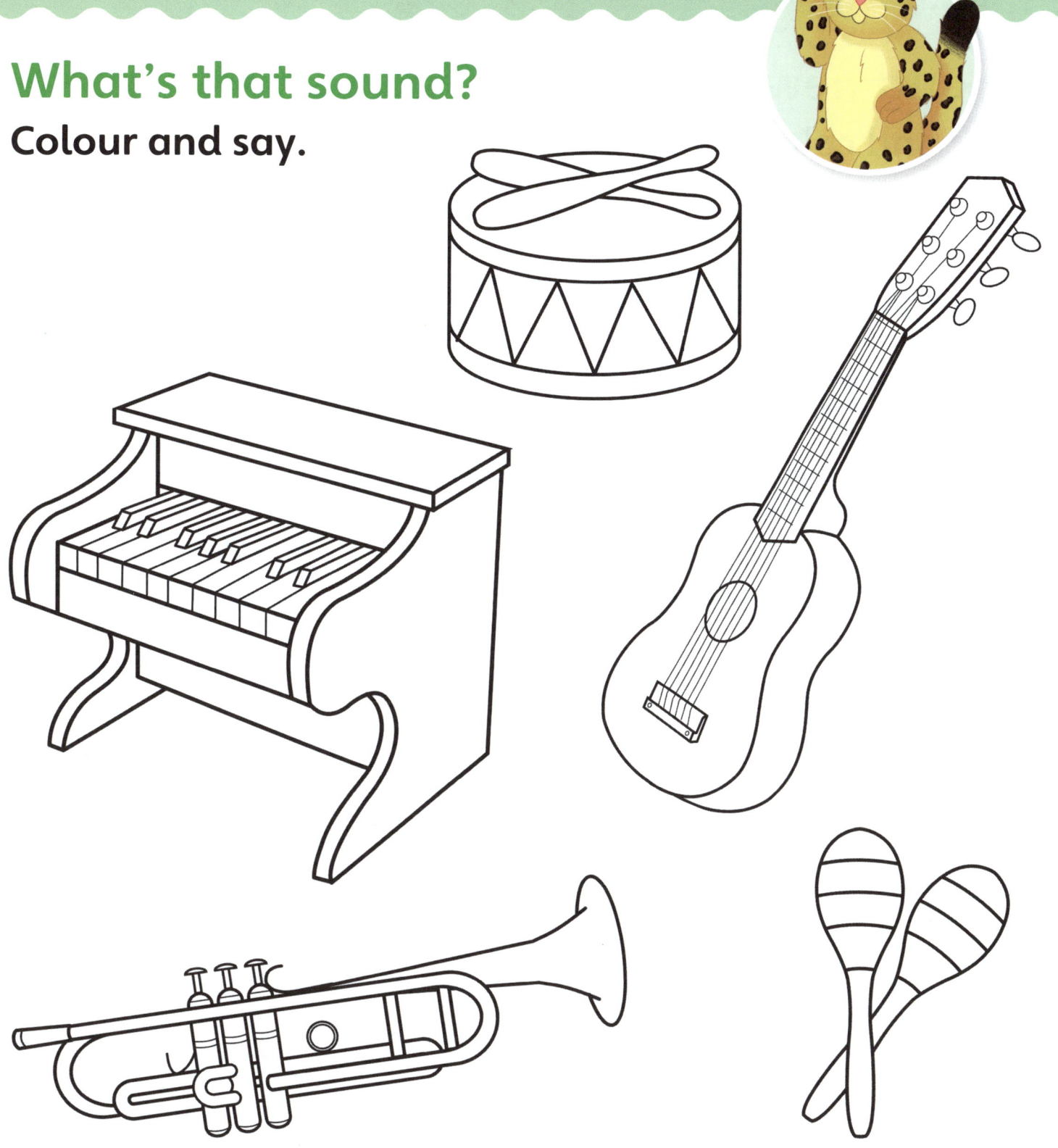

For practitioners
Children identify the instruments. Talk about the sound that each instrument makes, asking children to describe the sound. Remind them of the words strong/soft and high/low to help them. *Ask Can you make a loud/soft sound?* Then they can colour in the instruments.

Making new colours
Think and colour.

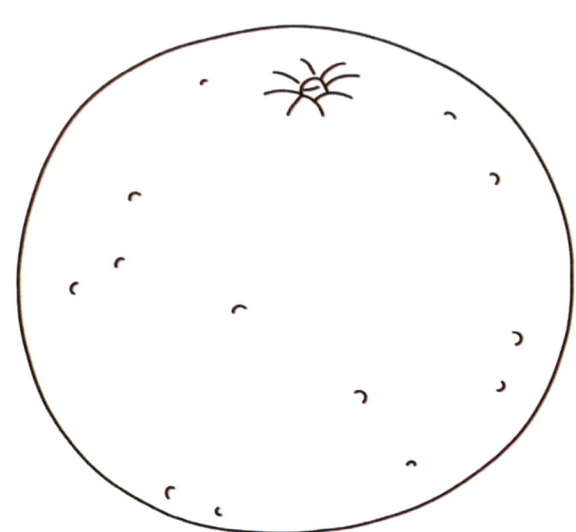

For practitioners
Ask What are these pictures of? What colour do you think they should be? Remind children of how we can mix yellow, red and blue to make new colours. Talk about the colour formulas and what colour these might make. Children then mix the primary colours as per the formulas to make new colours to fit the pictures. Children can also experiment with other colour combinations.

When I was one

Sing.
Act out each verse with sound effects.

We're going this way,
That way,
Forwards and backwards,
Over the great blue sea.
Let's have a run.
It's lots of fun.
A sailor's life for me!

When I was one,
I played the drums.
The day I went to sea,
I jumped onto
A big, big ship,
And the captain said to me:
(chorus)

When I was two,
I tied my shoe.
The day I went to sea,
I jumped onto
A big, big ship,
And the captain said to me:
(chorus)

When I was three,
I hurt my knee.
The day I went to sea,
I jumped onto
A big, big ship,
And the captain said to me:
(chorus)

When I was four,
I knocked on the door.
The day I went to sea,
I jumped onto
A big, big ship,
And the captain said to me:
(chorus)

When I was five,
I did a dive.
The day I went to sea,
I jumped onto
A big, big ship,
And the captain said to me:
(chorus)

For practitioners

Ask children to imagine they are a sailor on a ship. In pairs, children talk about each picture and what the characters are doing. Some children could sing the song while others join in making sound effects, e.g., splashing sounds for the verse *I did a dive*, and movements to match, taking on the character of the child in the song.

What is it?

Join the dots and colour.

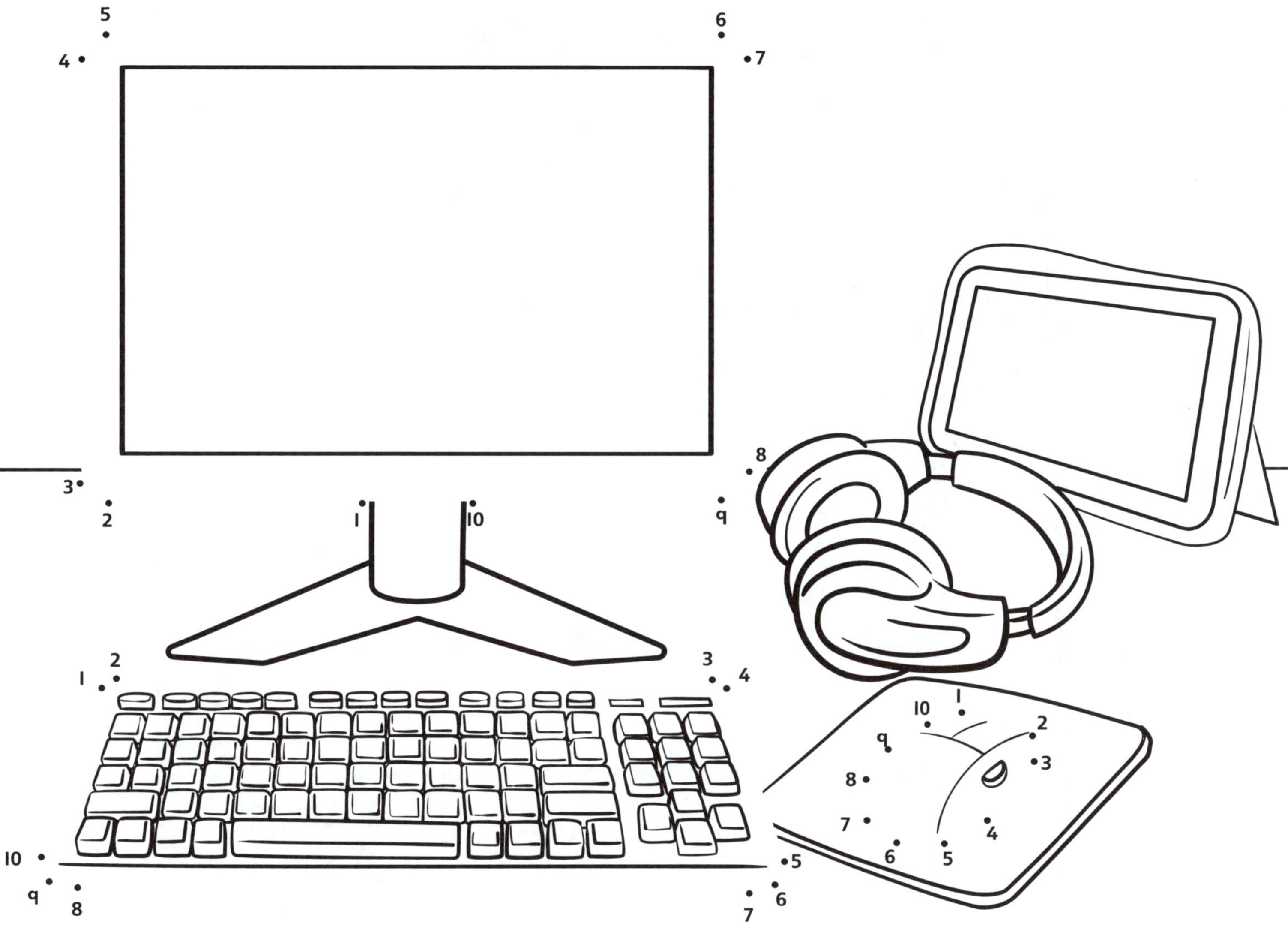

For practitioners

Children join the dots and add colour to complete the picture. Talk about the picture, asking children to name each digital device and piece of equipment, as well as what they might be used for. Ask *Have you seen or used any of this equipment? What have you used them for?*

Robot and cat

Think and draw.

For practitioners

Review the movement cards. Explain what each one means (they are not *forward*, *backward* and *turn*, they are *up*, *down*, *left* and *right*). Children move their own bodies in these directions to ensure they understand what each one means. Children then use the movement cards in order to navigate through the maze to reunite the robot and its cat. This mirrors the programming of toys, which you could also use if you have some. See if children can use the instruction cards to move a real programmable toy in the same way as the robot, as it completes the maze to find its cat.

Stickers for pages 4–5

Stickers for pages 18–19

Stickers for pages 22–23

Which do you like better?
Trace and say.

For practitioners
The photos represent things we have looked at in this topic. Children look at the pairs of photos and express which they liked best by filling in the heart next to their preferred activity. Encourage children to talk about each picture, for example, what it is, if they like it, who they did the activity with, and whether they have tried the activity with their family or friends outside of school.

Block 4 Wonderful water

How do we use water?
Choose stickers and say.

For practitioners
Children explore the picture and discuss what they can see. Children stick the matching pictures in place. Talk about how the families use water. Ask *How is water used in this picture? Why is it important to drink water?* Encourage children to find Gemi in the picture.

Staying dry!
Circle and talk.

For practitioners
Encourage children to say what each child is using to shelter from the rain and what it is made of e.g., a drawing made of paper. Ask children to think about what happens when each material gets wet. Is it waterproof? Will water run off it or go through it? Then ask children to work in pairs to circle who will get wet through. Discuss their answers.

It's raining!
Circle and draw.

For practitioners
Children discuss and circle the photos of clothes on the left that will keep them dry on a rainy day. Ask them to describe the materials these items are made from, and why those materials are good for a rainy day. Then children draw rain clothes of their choice on the person. These don't need to be perfect or look exact. Children talk about their choices, describing what items they have drawn and why.

Where do these animals live?

Choose stickers and say.

Place animal stickers in the water or on land.
Draw one more animal in the water.

For practitioners

Children discuss and decide whether each animal in the stickers lives in the water or on land. They then place the stickers in appropriate places and draw an additional animal that lives in the water. Encourage children to work with others and discuss their choices. Once finished, they can then make the sounds and movements of the animals in the picture.

What is missing?
Think and draw.

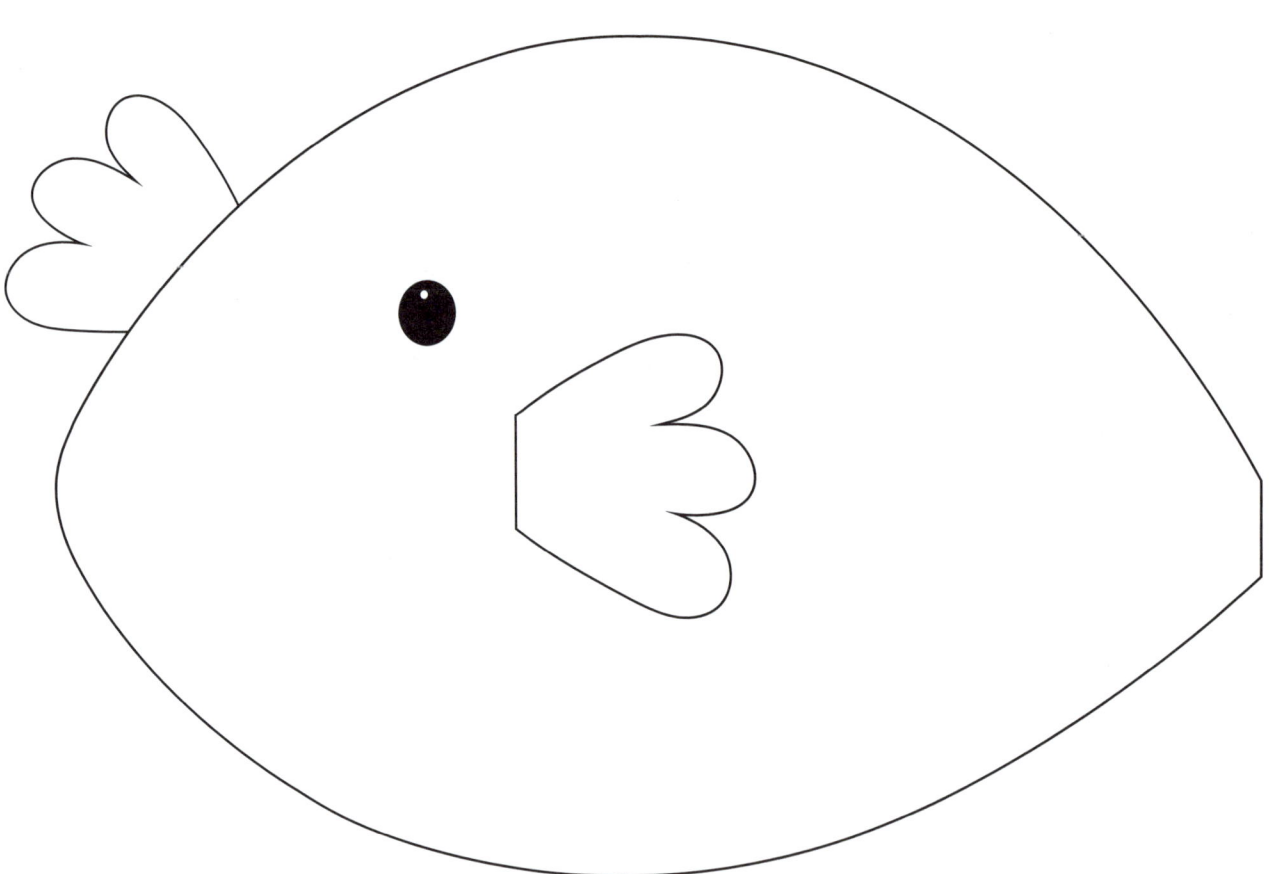

This fish has 2 eyes, 2 fins and a tail.

A duck has 2 eyes, 2 legs, 2 wings and a beak.

For practitioners

Read the sentence below each drawing with the children. Ask *What's missing?* Children draw the missing body parts. Ask *How do a fish and a duck look similar? How do they look different?* Encourage children to colour in the animals and add background.

Colourful fish!

Point and say.
Play with a partner.

For practitioners
Children describe their favourite fish. Model this by saying *My favourite fish is blue and white/spiky/spotty. Can you find it?* In pairs, children then take it in turns to describe a fish on the page. Their partner has to guess which fish they are describing and circle it. They take it in turns until all fish have been described and circled correctly. Make sure children are using different colour pens.

Bubbles Goes Home

Listen to the story.

Listen and act out Bubbles's adventure.

Bubbles the Octopus liked his keeper at the aquarium.

She gave him delicious food and interesting toys.

But Bubbles missed his home in the ocean.

One day, he saw a chance to go home.

Bubbles **twisted** and **pushed** and **pulled** until he was out of his tank.

He **slithered** across the floor and **squeezed** through a drainpipe.

The pipe was long and narrow.

SPLASH! Bubbles was back in the ocean.

He **stretched** out all 8 legs and felt the waves **rock** him.

Whoosh! Bubbles **shot** like a rocket through the water.

It felt wonderful to be free.

Bubbles **searched** for the perfect cave.

Hooray! An excellent cave for an octopus.

Bubbles **wiggled** inside. He was home.

For practitioners

Tell children that *Bubbles Goes Home* is based on a true story. Read each caption. Have children act out the movements described in the captions. For example, for Frame 3 ask *How did Bubbles get out of his tank?* As you read the text again, tell the children to listen to the action words and show you how Bubbles moved.

Trace Bubbles's journey
Draw and say.

For practitioners
Ask *What do you see? Can you find Bubbles's new home?* Encourage children to talk about how they think Bubbles feels now he is home and how his life is different compared to being in a tank. Ask children to move like an octopus in a small tank and then make big expressive movements to show how Bubbles might move now he is home in the ocean where he is happy. Children complete the maze.

Float or sink?
Circle.

Does it float or sink?		
✏️	float	sink
🖍️	float	sink
📄	float	sink
⭕	float	sink
🥄	float	sink

For practitioners
This activity can be completed at home or in class. You may provide materials (basin of water, pencil, crayon, small piece of paper, rubber band, spoon) to do this experiment as a whole class activity or for several small groups to use simultaneously. For each item ask children if it will float or sink. After guessing, have them try it out and record the results by circling the word float or sink.

Build a boat.
Draw.

This is my boat.

For practitioners
Ask children to think about what floats and what sinks. Encourage them to think about which materials are good choices for making a boat. Children can draw the boat they made during the class activity, or they can draw a new boat. Ask children what their boats are made of and whether they think they will float or sink. Why?

Acknowledgements

The authors and publishers acknowledge the following sources of copyright material and are grateful for the permissions granted.
While every effort has been made, it has not always been possible to identify the sources of all the material used, or to trace all copyright holders.
If any omissions are brought to our notice, we will be happy to include the appropriate acknowledgements on reprinting.

Thanks to the following for permission to reproduce images:

p6 gradyreese/GI, FG Trade/GI, South_agency/GI, miodrag ignjatovic/GI, Tom Werner/GI; p17 Adil Chelebiyev/GI, beekeepx/GI, skynesher/GI, Ariel Skelley/GI, Alexandr Screaghin/GI, mykeyruna/GI, Catherine Falls Commercial/GI, adventtr/GI; p21 Dorling Kindersley: Ruth Jenkinson/GI, jtyler/GI, Anna Valieva/GI, MirasWonderland/GI, malerapaso/GI; p22 (stickers) Ernesto r. Ageitos/GI, Quan Mahn/500px/GI, André Gilden/GI, Gary W. Carter/GI, Ornitolog82/GI; p26 abadonian/GI, KajaNi/GI, richcarey/GI, GlobalP/GI, Mirko_Rosenau/GI, GlobalP/GI, tane-mahuta/GI, lamyai/GI, alxpin/GI; p30 Ivantsov/GI, Garrett Aitken/GI, stockcam/GI, Alasdair James/GI, xenicx/GI

Key: GI = Getty Images

Thanks to the following artists at Beehive Illustration:

Lays Bittencourt, Tamara Joubert, Jo Litchfield, Michelle McGovern, Carl Pearce, Claire Philpott, Sarah Pitt, Elisa Rochi, Jan Smith.

Cover characters by Becky Davies (The Bright Agency)